BMW M4

BY NATHAN SOMMER

TORQUE™

Are you ready to take it to the extreme? Torque books thrust you into the action-packed world of sports, vehicles, mystery, and adventure. These books may include dirt, smoke, fire, and dangerous stunts.

WARNING: read at your own risk.

This edition first published in 2020 by Bellwether Media, Inc.

Library of Congress Cataloging-in-Publication Data

Names: Sommer, Nathan, author.
Title: BMW M4 / by Nathan Sommer.
Description: Minneapolis, MN : Bellwether Media, Inc., [2020] | Series: Torque. Car Crazy | Includes bibliographical references and index. | Audience: Age 7-12. | D
Identifiers: LCCN 2018057353 (print) | LCCN 2018057749 (ebook) | ISBN 9781618915504 (ebook) | ISBN 9781644870099 (hardcover : alk. paper)
Subjects: LCSH: BMW M automobiles–Juvenile literature.
Classification: LCC TL215.B57 (ebook) | LCC TL215.B57 S66 2020 (print) | DDC 629.222/2-dc23
LC record available at https://lccn.loc.gov/2018057353

Editor: Kate Moening Designer: Josh Brink

Printed in the United States of America, North Mankato, MN.

TABLE OF CONTENTS

THE OPEN ROAD

A BMW M4 turns onto an open country road. Here, the bold sports car can show its driver what it is really made of.

The driver steps on the gas. The M4 speeds to 60 miles (97 kilometers) per hour in just 4.1 seconds!

The roar of the M4's powerful engine is the only thing heard on the back road. The car's strong brakes keep it controlled as it rounds tight corners.

The M4 is made for everyday driving. But it also runs like a race car!

THE HISTORY OF BMW

BMW did not start out making cars. It began as an aircraft producer in 1916. After World War I, the German company began making motorcycles.

BMW motorcycle factory

THE BMW 501

IN 1952, BMW RELEASED ITS 501 MODEL. THE CAR WAS BIG ENOUGH FOR SIX PEOPLE! IT DID NOT SELL VERY WELL. BUT IT SHOWED PEOPLE THAT BMW MADE GOOD LUXURY CARS.

1929 BMW Dixi

BMW's first car **model** was the Dixi! It came out in 1929. But the company did not seriously enter the car business until the 1950s.

The 1962 BMW 1500 was BMW's first popular model. The 1500 made BMW a leader in sports cars!

1963 BMW 1500

THE WORLD'S BEST

BMW'S E30 M3 MODEL HAS WON MORE RACES THAN ANY OTHER TOURING CAR!

BMW E30 M3

BMW also had racing success. Its cars won many **Formula One** events and **touring races** during the early 1980s. BMW later bought other brands like Mini Cooper and Rolls Royce.

BMW M4

The BMW M4 was introduced at the 2014 North American International Auto Show. The M4 updated BMW's famed 3 Series car. The M4 is even more powerful!

2014 North American International Auto Show

coupe

convertible

The M4 soon became one of BMW's most popular models. The car comes as both a **coupe** and a **convertible**.

TECHNOLOGY AND GEAR

The M4's twin **turbocharged** engine was specially made for the car. The engine was built to get the most power from as few **cylinders** as possible. It takes the car to speeds of 174 miles (280 kilometers) per hour!

twin turbocharged engine

A sturdy **suspension system** gives the M4 smooth **handling**. Tough wheels and strong brakes keep this powerful car safely controlled.

The M4's ultra-light body is made partly of **carbon fiber**. Its wide, sleek frame makes it more steady. It also makes the car super **aerodynamic**.

LESS IS MORE

BMW BUILT THE M4 TO WEIGH AS LITTLE AS POSSIBLE. THE CARBON FIBER ROOF WEIGHS 11 POUNDS (5 KILOGRAMS) LESS THAN A STANDARD STEEL ROOF!

Its wide body and front grilles make the M4 stand out. A rear **spoiler** helps the car grip the road.

Inside, the M4 is packed with cool features. Buttons on the steering wheel let drivers control the suspension and **traction**. The car can remember different settings for different drivers.

The M4's leather seats have comfortable side cushions to keep passengers in place. Its armrests even have phone chargers!

2019 BMW M4 SPECIFICATIONS

CAR STYLE	COUPE OR CONVERTIBLE
ENGINE	TWINPOWER TURBO INLINE 6-CYLINDER
TOP SPEED	174 MILES (280 KILOMETERS) PER HOUR
0 - 60 TIME	UP TO 4.4 SECONDS
HORSEPOWER	425 HP (317 KILOWATTS) @ 5500-7300 RPM
CURB WEIGHT	UP TO 4,165 POUNDS (1,889 KILOGRAMS)
WIDTH	73.6 INCHES (187 CENTIMETERS)
LENGTH	184.5 INCHES (469 CENTIMETERS)
HEIGHT	54.4 INCHES (138 CENTIMETERS)
WHEEL SIZE	18 INCHES (46 CENTIMETERS)
COST	STARTS AT $69,150

TODAY AND THE FUTURE

BMW plans to keep the M4 around for a long time. The company wants to make the car bigger and even faster. It also wants the brakes and suspension to feel more like a race car's.

M4s are the perfect mix of speed and **luxury**. These powerful sports cars carry on BMW's history of excellence!

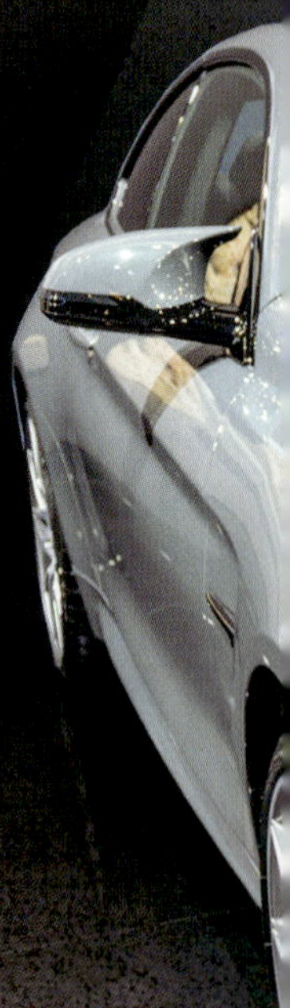

AN ICONIC LOGO

EVERY M4 COMES WITH BMW'S FAMOUS "M" LOGO ON ITS SEATS. THESE LIGHT UP WHEN THE CAR IS ON!

HOW TO SPOT A BMW M4

DEEP SIDE VENTS

POWER DOME HOOD

FRONT GRILLES

GLOSSARY

aerodynamic—having a shape that can move through the air quickly

carbon fiber—a strong, lightweight material made from woven pieces of carbon

convertible—a car with a folding or soft roof

coupe—a car with a hard roof and two doors

cylinders—parts in a car's engine that take gasoline and turn it into power

Formula One—a type of car racing

handling—how a car performs around turns

luxury—expensive and offering great comfort

model—a specific kind of car

spoiler—a part on the back of the car that helps the car grip the road

suspension system—a series of springs and shocks that help cars grip the road

touring races—races where amped-up versions of road cars compete against each other

traction—the force that helps cars grip the road

turbocharged—an engine with increased horsepower

TO LEARN MORE

AT THE LIBRARY

Doeden, Matt. *Sports Cars*. North Mankato, Minn.: Capstone Press, 2019.

Farndon, John. *Megafast Cars*. Minneapolis, Minn.: Hungry Tomato, 2016.

Lanier, Wendy Hinote. *Sports Cars*. Lake Elmo, Minn.: Focus Readers, 2017.

ON THE WEB

FACTSURFER

Factsurfer.com gives you a safe, fun way to find more information.

1. Go to www.factsurfer.com.

2. Enter "BMW M4" into the search box and click .

3. Select your book cover to see a list of related web sites.

INDEX

The images in this book are reproduced through the courtesy of: Jakub "Flyz1" Maciejewski, front cover; BMW newsroom, pp. 4-5, 6-7; ullstein bild Dtl/ Getty, p. 8; Roman Belogorodov, p. 9; Ralf Roletschek, p. 10; CJM Photography/ Alamy, p. 11; Steve Lagreca/ Alamy, p. 12; Joseph M. Arseneau, p. 13 (top); Ed Aldridge, p. 13 (bottom); Sergey Kuznetsov/ Alamy, p. 14 (top); PaulLP, p. 14 (bottom); Ronnie Ronnie/ Alamy, p. 15; bankerwin, p. 16; Zavatskiy Aleksandr, p. 17; Gargantiopa, p. 18; lev radin, p. 19; Sjoerd van der Wal/ Getty, pp. 20-21; Alina Fomenko, p. 21 (top left); Gregorz Czapski, p. 21 (top middle, top right).